THE IMPACT OF EXCELLENT CUSTOMER SERVICE ON BUSINESS GROWTH

Uche Akeeb

THE IMPACT OF EXCELLENT CUSTOMER SERVICE ON BUSINESS GROWTH

Copyright © 2018 by Uche Akeeb. All rights reserved.

No part of this book may be used or reproduced in any manner whatsoever without written permission from the publisher, except for brief quotations used in critical articles or reviews.

TABLE OF CONTENTS

PREFACE VI
ACKNOWLEDGEMENT IX
ABOUT THE AUTHOR XI
INTRODUCTION XII

1
EXCELLENT CUSTOMER SERVICE: HOW TO BE SUCCESSFUL AND PROFITABLE IN YOUR BUSINESS 1

2
HOW TO EFFECTIVELY DIFFUSE IRATE CUSTOMERS 17

3
HOW EXCELLENT CUSTOMER SERVICE CONVERTS ONE TIME BUYER INTO REPEAT CUSTOMERS 29

4
HOW TO AVOID EMOTIONAL MELTDOWN AND AVOID WEAK WORDS 47

5
IMPORTANCE OF EMPOWERING YOUR CUSTOMER CONTACT STAFF 57

CONCLUSION 65

REFERENCES 68

PREFACE

Customer service training should be an essential part of business strategy.

A lot of businesses tend to focus more on the product and forget to pay attention to the people who the product is made for. Providing excellent customer service is very important. The customer is the essence of your existence. You can have a great product and still fail because of not valuing your customer. There used to be a time when businesses define themselves to the customers but now customers define businesses to themselves.

Excellent customer service does not only lead to increased sales and improved returns (because your customers will return and bring new customers through referrals) but will also help companies stand out in this very competitive marketplace. Customer loyalty is priceless!

Put you customers first and you will be on the pathway to success.

I have the opportunity of being a Live Chat Solution Provider for a great company (Global Custom Commerce) and they have created an environment where one can thrive if you genuinely care about the customer. They realize that it is the skills and attitude of the customer service reps that makes the difference and I have learnt so much from this.

Having 15 years of customer service experience, I am very passionate about exceptional service, it gives me great fulfilment when I am able to diffuse an Irate customer or convert a one-time buyer into a repeat customer just because of my attitude towards them and I would not be happy to be treated less by the companies I patronize.

So, I would like businesses to recognize the effectiveness of excellent service to the success of the business and also, it is just a matter of common courtesy to value your customers and treat them exceptionally, because they are one of the main reasons for your growth, they deserve to be appreciated and treated with great value.

When the President of the Global African Business association appointed me to become the Business Specialist and Customer service trainer for GABA, it inspired me to share these principles and values with every entrepreneur and business organization that wants to know more on improving their customer service experience, which can lead to strengthening and contributing to the growth of any company even in a challenging economy.

Excellent service is a great tool every company should have. In this book, I explained the steps to follow, in order to constantly make exceptional service a habit for your company with my real life examples. Following these steps will give your company the opportunity to stand out in this very competitive marketplace. The main aim of this book is to provide guidance on adopting the ability to do it right by the customer and I want this book to have a great impact in customer service for a long time.

That's why I've kept it simple, short and relevant, to attract even those that do not enjoy reading a lot.

ACKNOWLEDGEMENT

I am very grateful to all the people who have researched on this topic because they have laid down the foundation and developed our knowledge. I am also grateful to Akindele Akiyemi, the president of GABA for inspiring this book.

I am grateful to Global Custom Commerce for helping me achieve what I never thought could be possible. To Jay Steinfeld, founder of Global Custom Commerce, your story inspire me a lot and it gives me hope.

To Steve O' Connor, President Global Custom Commerce, thank you for your genuine support and encouragement.

To Sarah Batalla, my trainer and manager who have trained me from the beginning to always seek to improve myself. To my Mum, for taking out time to review the content of this book, I appreciate you. To my wonderful friends turned sisters who always encourage me to pursue my dreams.

So grateful to my sister, Jennifer Harris for investing her time into creating my book cover.

To Oluyemi Adeyemi, for his great support and impact on my life's journey.

I want to thank my wonderful husband and lovely children for being my greatest inspiration.

I thank God, for making this possible!

ABOUT THE AUTHOR

Uche Akeeb is the Vice president of customer service for the Global African Business Association. She is also a customer service trainer with 15 years of customer service experience. She organizes seminars, workshops and teach entrepreneurs how to be successful and profitable in their businesses by offering exceptional customer service, a method which she constantly applies in everything she does and have been able to make over $1 million dollars in sales annually for Global Custom Commerce as a Live chat solution provider, for 3 years consecutively.

She is also the founder of Uchexclusive clothing line based in Katy, TX.

Her main goal is to get businesses to treat their clients in an exceptional way.

Uche Akeeb has been featured in print and broadcast outlets, including Afrocentrik TV, Voyage Houston, Authorvoices.com.

She is a first-class graduate from the University of Ibadan where she got her Bachelors degree in Economics.

She completely understands the effectiveness of excellent customer service towards the growth of a business. She enjoys serving people and love inspiring their transformation.

INTRODUCTION

Every thriving business today requires good customer service skills. It is important to keep existing customers as well as creating new ones. Customer service is the heart of the customers buying experience and businesses that provide great service to customers distinguish themselves among the rest in this very competitive world.

This is the main reason why many successful companies make this an important element in their agenda. Many businesses go out of their way and hire professionals with outstanding service oriented attitude to provide excellent customer service.

A disenchanted customer does not necessarily mean the business or the services received are a failure. The business may not have done something to make their customers fume at them, but something related to the business or service made that person mad.

It costs a lot more to attract new customers than to retain existing customers. Excellent customer service does not only lead to increased sales and improved returns (because your customers will return and bring new customers through referrals) but will also help companies stand out in this very competitive marketplace.

People often look for good treatment over good product and businesses should highly consider this since customers deserve to get their money's worth. According to online website Forbes, "Words alone are very powerful and they have a big influence on what your employees and customers think. If you don't set both of these groups' expectations up front, your company will never be able to excel in customer service"

Encouraging feedback within your organization is also a good call to make because not only do you foster openness, you also make others believe that you are there for their best interests. The article added that mistakes should be admitted. "Once you admit it, the customer will be happier"

Effective customer service is fundamental to success. But it's often forgotten or neglected. No matter what you're selling, business success is built on satisfying customers one at a time. It's about delivering great customer service.

Repeat business and referrals are fundamental to the maximum long-term growth and profitability on any enterprise. After all, repeat buyers and referrals are the most profitable sales you can possibly generate. If every customer is a one-time buyer only, you'll need to consistently fill the pipeline with fresh new prospects to make any sales at all. Providing exceptional customer service significantly increases the odds of subsequent purchases. You set yourself up to have customers buy from you again and again, without even considering other options.

As merchants, we need to bend over backwards to satisfy those who patronize our businesses. This means giving the customer the benefit of any doubt. Provide the kind of courtesy, attentiveness and service you expect and are entitled to when you're the buyer. It's the Golden Rule applied to business. Play the role of the buyer and upgrade your customer service accordingly.

Nobody wants an unsatisfied customer unless they're not worth having. Thankfully, this is rare, though problem customers are out there. If you've been in business for any length of time, you've probably experienced the "impossible to satisfy" customer.

No reasonable businessperson wants their name and reputation dragged through the mud. The easiest way to prevent this kind of occurrence is to take extra care of those you serve.

The worst thing any business owner can do is to not respond to emails and phone calls. Ignoring calls only makes matters worse as customers feel neglected or abandoned - usually after spending a fair amount of cash on your product or service. When ignored repeatedly, a disappointed customer's frustration and stress level can build to the boiling point. And that's exactly what you want to avoid at all costs.

Also, when you respond, ensure that it is in a timely manner. Consumers get frustrated when they run into issues and their problem is not resolved in a timely manner. Response time is very essential. Ensure your customers are getting the help they need in a timely manner and create a positive impression on your product/brand.

1

EXCELLENT CUSTOMER SERVICE: HOW TO BE SUCCESSFUL AND PROFITABLE IN YOUR BUSINESS

Disregard the title on your business card. That's right, whatever title you currently have, disregard it.

No matter what your titled position is designated as, you are in customer service.

Everyone in your organization is serving the customer. Even those who work behind the scenes and never come face to face with the customer bringing in the dollars are working to support those who do.

The person who answers the phone, the person who distributes mail, the person making purchasing decisions, the person managing projects, the person providing janitorial services - all of these people are performing functions that ultimately impact the paying customer in some form or fashion. The trick is to make sure that all of these individuals recognize that they are not working independently, but as a team to benefit the customer.

The main reason customers leave? You and your treatment of them.

Customers are leaving your business mainly because of how you treat them. The number one reason cited 70% of the time for leaving a place of business is based solely on the experience that you provided. Consumers today are delighted when they are treated as valued partners in the business and are not processed through the system. When businesses practice the basic concept of courtesy and good manners, customers notice it and come back for more. Customers are hungry for businesses that welcome them into their place of business, that greet them warmly, make eye contact (for businesses that are not online only), introduce themselves, offer assistance when needed. They enjoy the experience so much more when they are thanked for their business at the end of the transaction are encouraged and invited to come back again.

Too often, customers are treated as a nuisance or necessary evil of running the business. They are seen as time wasters. While we all have had the occasional bad day and don't want to interact with another customer, we need to recognize that those very customers are the ones sustaining our business.

If you don't serve your customers well, someone else will.

The smart companies are those that are focusing on their customers and looking for ways to serve them well. The customer is the sole determining factor in the success of your business. Customers are recognizing this fact and are looking for those businesses that deliver excellent customer service. They want to do business with those that effectively manage the customer experience.

It's all about Customer Experience Management.

Delivering excellent customer service involves all aspects of the customer experience. It starts from the initial desire of your product or service on the part of the customer and extends through every customer contact point, to the point of follow up after the transaction. When this process is well managed with the customer's benefit as the focal point, the entire company has then become customer centric and started to build the relationship that customers are craving from those they do business with.

By making sure that it is the customer and their needs that you are serving, you are working in the best interest of both the customer and your business.

The Core skills to providing excellent customer service are:

- Greeting
- Product Knowledge
- listening Skills
- Setting the right expectation
- Be firm and consistent
- Acknowledge Customer's information.

GREETING: "Be the company that always honors people first." Jeanne Bliss.

Do not underestimate the power of greeting. The beginning of your conversation with your customer sets the tone for the entire conversation. They can feed off your energy.

Most times, Customer Service is the first point of contact and how you interact with the customer can make a difference in determining the success of the sale, having a satisfied customer and converting them into a repeat customer.

For face-to-face interaction, you greet with a beautiful smile.

Over the phone, you will also smile and greet with a lively tone, your smile can also be felt over the phone. Even when they are very upset, hearing your lively tone and sincere greeting can help calm them and result into a positive experience.

Welcome to ……., Thank you for calling…… are some words you should use generously. A positive greeting will make the customer comfortable in explaining their needs, which can lead to making a sale.

PRODUCT KNOWLEDGE: Product knowledge is a very important skill that can lead to increased sales. Even if you don't know 100% about the product, it's worth it to take the time to know your product extensively. This helps you create value for the product you are selling, gives you confidence, and enable you ask the right questions, in order to provide your customer with the right solution.

Every company has a purpose of solving a specific problem and product knowledge helps you to focus on what the customers needs.

I remember when a customer called me and was excited about getting the solar shades for her new home. I replied, "Congratulations on your new home! I'm happy to assist you in placing an order for the solar shades but in order to best assist, I need to ask you a few questions, okay?"

I then proceeded to ask her what she loved about the solar shades, she explained to me that she loves how she goes to Starbucks and can see out but no one can see in. I let her know that, at night when the lights are on, people can see in too and she has bedrooms and bathrooms that needs privacy. This made her to take a pause, she never thought of it.

At the end of the day, I provided her with options that will enable her to see out and still provide privacy at night. This was a large order, if she had gotten the solar shades and installed them, she would have realized this by the time she receives the shade and would be so frustrated. And guess who she would blame for it? Me.

Guess who is at fault if that had happened?......... Meeee. Why is this? Simply because I am the expert and should be the one to educate her on our product features, ask the right questions and provide her with the best solution for her needs. I had a satisfied customer at the end of this call.

When you create value, customer get excited to buy the product.

LISTENING SKILLS: Customers Want to Truly be Heard and Understood. It is very important to take time to stop and listen to everything the customer says.

Sometimes, it can be challenging to do this, when you hear some key words and it's taking too long for them to explain a situation or what they want. Being that you are the expert, it can be tempting for you to assume that you understand, before allowing them completely finish their statement. Your assumption can be wrong and if this is the case, it delays the solution process, leading to an unpleasant experience.

Patience is the key here. Stop to completely listen, ask questions to confirm you understand what they are saying and confirm everything they said in your own words, the best way you can. This will ensure you are both on the same page, save time and create a pleasant experience for the customer.

Always confirm with the customer, they are happy when they know the communication is going smoothly and they are being heard and understood.

I had a customer who called and confidently told me she needed a replacement control pole for her blind. While reviewing the order, I saw she had the faux wood blind which uses a tilt rod and a control pole. I could have easily assumed she understood what she needed and immediately ordered the replacement pole she needed but I asked, "just to confirm, you need the control pole that is attached to the pull ring which you use to raise and lower the blinds, correct?" At this time, she replied No and explained that she needed the control pole that attached to the other side which is used to open and close the louvers.

This was when I realized she needed the tilt wand for twisting the louvers open and close, and ordered the correct part for her.

Pausing to ask the right question and listening to her reply, helped me offer the right solution. Receiving the wrong part would have made her frustrated and created an unpleasant experience and I am glad I was able to reverse that.

When you make good listening become a habit, you can easily reverse anything that could have created a bad experience for the customer and always proffer the right solution.

SETTING THE RIGHT EXPECTATION: This is very essential to gaining your customers' trust. It is best to under promise and over deliver.

Do not tell customers that they will receive a product in 3 days when you know it will get to them in 4 days. You might think the 1 day difference does not matter, however, when this becomes a habit, customers will lose their trust for your brand.

When you realize that the expectation you set are not being met, you need to quickly adjust the set expectation to match your reality.

There will be times when you will not be able to meet the set expectations, due to circumstances beyond your control, acknowledge this and apologize to the customer. Be truthful and honest with them about the situation, explain to them why the expectation was not met and let them know what you are doing to make things right.

Whenever I tell my customers I will follow up with them within 24 hours, I always do. Even if I do not have a solution for their situation yet, I still follow up to let them know I am working towards getting a solution. The most important thing is that I keep to my promise.

Transparency helps to meet and exceed customer's expectations, increasing repeat customers and referrals. Can also create lifetime value for your brand/ product.

BE FIRM AND CONSISTENT: Consistency is a very powerful tool in building customer's loyalty. Customers pay attention to every detail. It is essential to ensure that everyone representing your brand understands the way you want your customers to be treated, so that when your customer interacts with different people at different times, they get the same experience. Though, personalities differ, but when the practice is the same, the similarities can be detected.

Do not treat customers according to your mood at different times, it should be consistent every time and even better as you continuously improve.

Train your customer service representatives or anyone who is representing your brand with the same curriculum to maintain a consistent brand representation. This will ensure they develop strong practices and apply them to every customer interaction. When customers find that they receive the same high-quality service whenever they contact your company, they will see your company as reliable.

"Customers value consistency from their service providers because they base their expectations on previous positive experiences. Therefore, it is crucial to not only deliver good customer service at first asking but to keep on delivering service at the same, if not better, level every time, if you are to continue ensuring customer satisfaction." Dylon Mills.

*Acknowledge Customer's information: Do not overlook some important events that customer mentions to you. For example: "I just bought a new home and I would love to order blinds……." Going straight without acknowledging the great accomplishment of purchasing a new home, is not the best option. A good reply will be "Congratulations on your home! I am happy to assist with getting your blinds ordered………."

The customer did not mention it for you to notice it, they might have said this to make you understand their situation or what they want, but your attention to it will make the customer comfortable with you and make them believe that you truly care about their project and are willing to assist.

Come to think of it, how do you genuinely assist someone when you do not care about these little things? Pay attention to every detail, no matter how little it may seem, it will go a long way.

There are other minor skills that you can inculcate which will enable you make it easy all the time for your customer and deliver that Wow service.

One of them is: using simple terms to make your customer fully understand what you are trying to communicate. Sometimes, we are tempted to use unique terms that relates to our business, with the thought that it will impress your customer and make them feel you know your product. Or it just might be a habit because you are used to your product. If the customer does not understand the term you are using, it can be frustrating because they want to get the problem solved in a timely manner without having to ask you, "what do you mean by ………?"

We are the experts and understand our terms, if the customer is not in your line of business, they might not know several terms, so it is best to save everyone the time and always keep it simple for better and easy understanding.

2

HOW TO EFFECTIVELY DIFFUSE IRATE CUSTOMERS

No matter how good you are at what you do, what business you are in, or where it is located you will at some point find yourself facing an irate customer. Maybe a product was flawed, a delivery was late, or a charge was inaccurate. How you deal with that customer not only will determine how he or she feels about your organization, but how you feel about yourself.

When you are able to turn an irate customer into a satisfied customer, you will gain confidence in your ability to diffuse a volatile situation and to evoke a positive outcome.

When most people come in contact with an irate customer, their first instinct is to turn and run. Dealing with a customer who has a problem and is upset about it, can be more than a little daunting. With the proper perspective, however, you will see that the customer's complain is actually an opportunity for you and your organization to put your best foot forward.

Customers who have complaints are a blessing in disguise. They are letting you know where you and your organization have flaws and providing you with the opportunity to correct them. When you do, you will realize increased customer loyalty, revenues, and profits. It's a win/win situation.

You should be more concerned with the customers who don't complain than with those who do. In a recent study of retail banks in the United Kingdom, conducted by J.D. Power and Associates, results showed that while incentives are important in attracting new customers, customer service is key to retaining those customers. Almost 40 percent of customers left their banks because of a poor service experience, and an additional 43 percent cited poor service as a top reasons for intending to leave their banks.

Customer service is key to success of any business. Dealing with irate customers and solving their problems is a critical element of that service.

When dealing with an irate customer, take these steps:

Listen carefully and with interest to what the customer is telling you.

Empathize without laying blame, if they are at fault. Apologize if your company is at fault.

Put yourself in the customer's place, and respond in a way that shows you care about his or her concerns. Use phrases such as, "I understand that must be upsetting," or "I don't blame you for being upset; I would feel the same way."

Ask pertinent questions in a caring, concerned manner, and actively listen to the answers.

Suggest one or more alternatives that would address the customer's concerns.

Solve the problem quickly and efficiently, or find someone who can.

Using these steps will quickly calm most unhappy or angry customers and allow you to address and solve their problems. Patience and tact are key.

It's important that, even if a customer is making outrageous statements and, in essence, throwing a fit, that you remain calm. Do not take those statements personally. Apologize, take ownership, and empathize with the customer, then solve the problem.

Just as important as what you should do, there are five things you should not do:

Don't directly challenge someone who has a complaint and is angry. Even if that customer is wrong don't attempt to prove it. Your goal is to solve the problem, not to enter into a debate on the merits of the complaint.

Don't let the conversation wander or get off the topic. Solve the crisis at hand without looking for, and finding, additional problems.

Don't participate in fault finding. Shifting blame doesn't help anyone.

Do not interrupt them when they are talking. Wait for them to finish everything they have to say before you start talking. Allow them to let it all out. Sometimes, they just want to be heard and have the feeling that their complaints are valid.

Don't let your personal feelings get in the way. Stay cool and use courtesy and tact to diffuse the situation.

When you successfully handle irate customers and their complaints, you will be rewarded with a satisfied customer and a customer who will be loyal to you and your organization. That loyalty will have a positive impact on your organization's bottom line and make you look like a hero.

If dealing with irate customers makes you want to drive home, jump back into bed, and hide under the covers ... take heart. Once you know the tricks of the trade, angry customers become less upsetting and more acceptable as part of the customer service landscape. Here's how to diffuse overheated situations and win them over.

LISTEN FIRST, SPEAK LATER

The initial burst of anger from your customer will almost always be the most intense. And because it's so stressful for the person on the receiving end, flustered employees often try to end the confrontation quickly in order to ease their own discomfort. This mistake usually leads to escalation.

Resist the urge to interrupt, argue, or engage in problem solving. Instead, relax, slow down your breathing, and listen intently while nodding and making eye contact (for physical interaction) with your customer. For phone interaction, use acknowledging words like: ok, got it, I understand to confirm with them that you are listening.

APOLOGIZE AND EMPATHIZE

Your customer will eventually run out of steam and pause to collect his or her thoughts. When this happens, take the opportunity to apologize. An effective apology goes to the heart of what has upset your customer. For example, a customer who is displeased about an undisclosed $10 service charge is more likely to be angry about feeling deceived than about the fee itself. Address that anger specifically and empathize with it.

Example: "I'm sorry. That charge should have been pointed out to you at the time of your purchase. No one likes to be surprised by hidden fees."

Resist "blame shifting" or passing the buck. In your customer's eyes, you are the company, so don't take anything that's said to you personally. This is the secret to coping well with any customer service complaint.

CLARIFY

Immediately after apologizing, repeat the customer's complaint to him or her. Clarifying the complaint assures the customer that you're concerned about the problem and helps you avoid further misunderstandings that may reignite his or her anger again.

MAINTAIN A CALM, POSITIVE TONE

You have tremendous influence over your customer's emotional state. (Although it doesn't feel that way!) Lowering your voice and speaking slowly and calmly in a pleasant manner relaxes and disarms an angry customer.

TAKE IMMEDIATE ACTION

The longer they wait, the more they get upset. Make the unhappy customer your top priority. You want him or her to see you as an advocate, not an opponent. Begin working towards a solution. If you can't find an immediate answer or solution, take the lead in phoning the customer back. Jot down contact information and outline the corrective steps you will be taking. Include the names of everyone who will be involved in the solution.

One of the biggest drivers of customer's anger is feeling like they're getting the runaround.

Taking the steps above assures your customer of the following facts:

- He or she is valued.
- You have a plan.
- He or she won't be abandoned.
- You will be accountable and available for follow-up.

However, No one is superhuman. An unusually stressful incident involving an angry customer can leave you rattled. If a violent or near-violent incident took place, you certainly may benefit from support, even if it is just talking about it. If a stressful incident leaves you lacking energy or a positive attitude, contact your employee assistance program for practical tips and targeted help.

FOLLOW UP "TOUGH CASES"

An angry customer is not necessarily a former customer. So, don't write them off! A follow-up phone call or message a few days following the resolution of a complaint sends the message that you care about your customer's satisfaction and well-being. Most customers just want to feel valued. This technique builds super strong loyalty. You can't please everyone, but you can improve and enhance your company's image and responsiveness in every dispute. The more you practice these techniques, the more success you'll have calming customers, winning them over, and reducing stress.

UCHE AKEEB

3

HOW EXCELLENT CUSTOMER SERVICE CONVERTS ONE TIME BUYER INTO REPEAT CUSTOMERS

Repeat buyers might make up just 8% of visitors, but deliver a whopping of over 40% of revenue making them a lucrative segment of customers. Unfortunately, long-term, profitable customer relationships don't happen overnight. By investing in customer retention from the start, you can dramatically grow your bottom line while transforming one-time buyers into committed brand enthusiasts.

Taking new customers from their first purchase to their second can be a hurdle. But with each additional purchase, you can be more and more confident that your customer is here to stay. In fact, customers who have made two purchases in the past are nine times more likely to convert than new shoppers.

In this section, you'll learn how to inspire your customer to develop a purchasing habit. To accomplish this goal, you must help your customers integrate your brand into their daily routines.

Many people wrongly assume that repeat buyers are loyal customers. In reality, loyalty has very little to do with your customer's purchasing behavior. It's more about creating a connection between your brand and your customer.

THE IMPACT OF EXCELLENT CUSTOMER SERVICE ON BUSINESS GROWTH

In this section, you'll learn how to enhance your customer's commitment to your brand. To accomplish this goal, you must develop brand affinity between you and your customers.

What is the best way to gain users when it comes to ecommerce stores? Offer discounts and the consumers will come flocking to your website. Almost all ecommerce stores use this set rule to increase their user base and sales. However, by doing so, they are just eating into their resources and might be incurring losses. While they do end up increasing the buyers on their website, it eventually gets nothing to a business if those one-time buyers do not convert into repeat buyers.

You can't afford to attract buyers each day for routine sales. It's tiring and on the top of that, financially exhausting. Financially, because then you will have to spend a big chunk of your earnings on marketing like a newly setup business.

Let us look at one example:

I had a customer who had ordered blinds but the delivery was delayed because he ordered them during the festive season and the factory got swamped with more than expected order volume which led to a manufacturing back log . This customer had ordered them very close to the time he would be needing them, he wanted them to be installed before thanksgiving because he was having guests coming over for thanksgiving but as a result of the delay, the blinds would not be there before thanksgiving. It was delayed for 3 working days.

When he chatted in , he was so frustrated and upset, expressing how disappointed he was and how he would no longer purchase from us anymore. Putting myself in his shoes, I would be upset too. I let him get it all out and then I apologized for the delay, owned up to the fact that we disappointed him with the time frame, at this point he was ready to listen to me, then I went on to explain to him about the manufacturing back log, that all the dates we stated are estimated and sometimes situations beyond our control can lead to a little delay. I also suggested some options to cover his windows while his guests were around. I got approval from my manager to credit him back some money, so he could get some temporary shades from home depot to cover his windows, I informed him that some of the temporary shades look good, they give complete privacy and they have some of them that are blackout for the bedroom, and don't cost much, warning him that he might get stuck and not want to remove them from the window because of how good they look. We even laughed over it and before he got off the chat, he apologized for the way he spoke to me earlier, explaining that the pressure of everything (preparation for the arrival of his guests) got to him. He also assured me that he is sure coming back to get some shades for his vacation home from us.

Some customers might already be under pressure and then any little thing compounds their situation , as a result, they unload all of it on you, you just have to understand that it is nothing personal, with the right attitude, listening to them and owning up to any unfulfilled commitment or unintentional error that your organization has made, it will make the situation better for the customer. Sometimes, they just want to be heard. You have to be always genuinely care about solving the customer's problem.

It also gives me fulfilment whenever I get off these chats, knowing that I provided the right solution for the customer.

SO WHAT IS THE SOLUTION?

To make sure that the losses do not pile up, or that you do not go over your advertising budget, an online store must ensure that those acquired customers become repeat or lifetime customers. The bottom line is that most of these customers came to your website because you were offering discounts; thereby influencing their purchase decision. But you cannot go on giving discounts just to retain them.

The best possible way to retain their loyalty towards your store is to ensure that they remain interested in your products and services rather than the price that you offer. Let us throw some light on how to achieve such things:

Email marketing: Email, after social media, is by far one of the most powerful ways to stay in touch with target customers. It helps you develop a relationship with your customer and keeps them engaged. Most of the times, people forget about an online store after making their first purchase. Using email, you can keep reminding them about your store and the product that they might be interested in.

Remarketing: It is crucial to understand that if you blast your customer with regular emails, poking them every now and then, you are bound to end in their spam folder. In that scenario, you should use dynamic remarketing ads to maintain a level of visibility without seeming like a stalker.

Loyalty programs for repeat customers: Reward based programs have always been highly fruitful in ensuring the loyalty of customers. For example, let's say you own a coffee shop. And you tell your customers that after buying 5 cups of coffee the sixth coffee will be free. This will enable the customer to keep coming back to your coffee shop. Another example is when ecommerce store gives X discount on the purchase of over Y amount.

OFFER A GREAT PRODUCT EVERY TIME

Product inconsistency is a red flag for your customers. If the quality isn't consistent, you lose trust from your buyers, which isn't good news for your business. Guidelines, training, and a clear set of standards ensure every customer gets the same fantastic experience each time.

TRAIN EACH NEW EMPLOYEE PROPERLY

While time is often a resource we simply don't have enough of, training is essential for each and every new staff member. Proper training allows your team to understand the process and execute their job to the best of their abilities. This also allows the new hire to get familiar with the business and sets standards for quality, service, and presentation.

EMPOWER FOR YOUR STAFF WITH GUIDELINES

There should be Guidelines and directions that will help guide your team through daily tasks and situations in case you aren't there to field a question. It also helps ensure consistency. Take a restaurant, for example. Each chef needs to know the exact measurements and ingredients to make a meal taste the same every time so a hard copy recipe needs to be available for reference.

CONTINUOUS GROUP TRAININGS

Your employees shouldn't stop learning after being hired. Continuous Group trainings make sure everyone is on the same page and create a space for questions to be answered.

Learning as a group throughout the year keeps skills fresh, betters communication, and is an opportunity to learn something new.

PROVIDE EXCELLENT CUSTOMER SERVICE

Each and every customer deserves to be provided with a high level of customer service because it's just as important as the product itself. Going above and beyond should be leveraged from the local perspective, as this personal touch is something you can provide in greater quality and quantity than a big box store.

So much of exceptional day-to-day service comes down to tone: "Is there anything else I can assist you with?" and "What else do you want?" are in essence, asking the same thing, but are wildly different in terms of tone. In other words, great service not only depends on execution (that you asked in the first place), it also depends on perception, or how you communicated with the customer. Getting that right is the first step in building a business people love interacting with.

If you doubt the power of great service, keep these stats in mind:

89% of customers have stopped doing business with a company because of bad customer service.

It takes 12 positive customer experiences to make up for one negative experience.

70% of buying experiences are based on how the customer feels they are being treated.

How to do it? A few foolproof tips:

GREET YOUR CUSTOMERS BY NAME

It feels good to be remembered, doesn't it? Recalling your customer's name is an easy way to impress your customer and let him/her know you value their presence.

REMEMBER REPEAT ORDERS

There's nothing better than being able to walk into a business and be asked, "The regular?" Even if you have to keep a cheat sheet, this tool is an easy way to make your customers feel special.

BUILD RELATIONSHIPS

Remember names and orders, but don't be afraid to take it a step further and learn a bit more about your customers. Ask questions like, "Where are you from?" and "Have any family in the area?" to build rapport and relationships with your customers. This also provides content for future conversations.

MAKE EXCEPTIONS

As a local business, you have the power to bend the rules a bit to keep your customers happy. If someone asks for an item or a variation - you can grant that wish, if possible and you're willing.

THINK OF THE LITTLE THINGS

If you sell cupcakes, why not throw in some extra birthday candles? It's the little details that make a big difference.

Follow up with thank you note: When a user makes a first purchase on your website, it is always advised to follow up with a personalized and meaningful thank you email. This will make them feel special and let them know their importance.

Entice non-returning users with special discounts: One thing to note is that if a user has made a purchase on your website, there is definitely some way of making that one-time buyer into returning customer. A simple way is to entice that particular customer by offering a discount coupon for making a purchase.

Provide better customer service than the competition: When it comes to guaranteeing the loyalty of customers towards your product, nothing beats providing the best customer service. Always ensure that you go the extra mile while serving a customer. This includes delivery or any grievance redressal. In the end, if your customer service is above par the competition, then you can even justify premium prices.

Highlight previous customer experiences to new customers: Trust is a major factor in the current times based on which, users generally associate with brands and online businesses. When it comes to ecommerce marketplaces, the positive review and testimonials can do wonders for the store. By prominently highlighting on the website as well as social media profiles the positive experiences of your previous customers, you can easily win their trust and make sure that they convert into repeat customers.

The bottom line is that it is far easy to find one time buyers, but highly difficult to convert them into repeat customers. Most of the ecommerce stores think that if they get buyers on their platform, they will be successful. This is where they confuse between one-time buyers and repeat customers. In order to grow, you ought to focus on customer lifetime value.

Just doling out discounts in order to retain customers is never a sound business model. You need to engage with your audience and incorporate the above-mentioned strategies to capture their interest, enabling them to come back to your store for new purchases.

HAVING A SOLID PRESENTATION

This one seems like a no-brainer, but keeping your business clean, visually appealing, and in tip-top shape is extremely important. Your business's presentation is a reflection of the products being offered.

HIRE CLEANING HELP

For Brick and mortar stores, If you don't have time to do a deep clean regularly, hire a cleaning service to come weekly or monthly to do the intensive scrub-down and cobweb snatching.

REPLACE BURNT-OUT LIGHTS

Lighting on both the interior and exterior of your building (signage included) should be fully functional.

KEEP RESTROOMS CLEAN

Clean restrooms are more than functional, ensure they're stocked with toiletries and are funk free.

REMOVE STAINS

Stains on walls, carpeting, ceilings and furniture will make your business look sloppy and dated.

ORGANIZE

Keep your office(s) tidy with filing systems and proper storage.

If your business can convert first-time customers into forever customers, you're golden. These loyal supporters will be a referral engine, and your high standards for the products, service, and presentation of your business will continue to impress new customers, keeping the traffic flow steady through your front door.

UCHE AKEEB

4

HOW TO AVOID EMOTIONAL MELTDOWN AND AVOID WEAK WORDS

Gone are the days where customer transactions only transpire in person or over the phone. There's now livechat, social media and email form of communication with customers.

These days, the modern customer expects help on their terms whether that be via social media or a messaging app, during standard work hours or in the middle of the night.

And they expect that help to be just that helpful. They want the person on the other end of the line (or screen, or app) to get to the root of the problem fast, and provide a solution even faster.

But there are a few things that can cause the conversation to take a wrong turn, including the customer service phrases below.

1. Let Me Look Into That

When helping a customer work through a problem, you really want to flex your direct communication skills. This isn't to say you should be insensitive or argumentative, but rather you should aim to: Set expectations. Are you going to put them on hold while you dig in? How long do you expect this to take? Be upfront.

Define your plan of action. What exactly are you looking into? Are you going to check their account information? Ask a colleague? Let them know you actually have a plan and you're not just scrambling.

With this in mind, you might say something more specific like, "This is possible, but I need to run a report first. This will only take two or three minutes, do you mind if I place you on hold while I process it?"

2. Unfortunately, No

You might be thinking, "Is there really a good way to say 'no'?"

Turns out, there are ways to soften the blow and provide a better experience for the customer, even when you can't accommodate their request entirely.

Instead of leading with the negative, try offering up the best possible alternative first -- it may end up being just what they need.

Can't think of an alternative right off the bat? Try asking a few clarifying questions first.

By drawing out more detail, you may find that there is, in fact, a way to offer them support -- or at least meet them in the middle.

An example of a better way to say No: "I would really love to …., however……. (then explain why you are not able to grant their demands at that time)"

3. There's Nothing I Can Do

This is a comeback that customer service and customer success professionals fall back on when they are limited by policies and protocol, which the business organization has in place.

To combat this, it's important to first surface this as a concern to senior management, as the decision to remove or reduce restrictive policies typically falls in their court.

If there's no wiggle room to reduce policies and protocol, this phrase is still inexcusable and there's always something you can do, even if it's just listening, empathizing and explaining in details why you are not able to give what they are asking. This might help them better understand why their demands cannot be met.

4. Let Me Correct You on That

But, but, the customer is always right, correct?

When dealing with a situation where a customer is misunderstanding the way something works, take a minute to remember that you've made mistakes before too and this is not the time and place to flex your authority or come off as accusatory.

Instead, employ a helpful tone and say something like, "Let's take a look at this issue together and see what we can do."

Apple has gone as far as creating a rule against employees correcting customer mispronunciations, as they feel it's both condescending and rude to do so,

according to an article from Business Insider.

5. There Must've Been A Miscommunication

Giving and receiving information isn't always easy, especially when the customer is feeling frustrated or confused.

Rather than allowing emotions to muddy up your communication, take accountability for ensuring that the customer fully understands the situation and all of the possible outcomes.

What's obvious to you, might not be so obvious to someone lacking proper context. This might mean that you need to adjust your communication style to ensure that you're clearly stating your intentions and conveying your willingness to help, regardless of any confusion that may have taken place.

6. I'm Sorry, I'm Sorry, I'm Sorry

The phrase "I'm sorry" is often used as a crutch phrase, one that carries little significance or impact when used out of context.

In other words:

Don't say sorry when you really mean, "I'll have to look that up."

Don't say sorry when you really mean, "Can I ask you a question?"

Don't say sorry when you really mean, "I want to understand the problem better."

And if you are going to apologize, follow it up with a solution. Customers want to know that you're actually going to do something about the mistake or miscommunication.

7. I Have Another Call Coming In, Can You Hang On

No customer wants to be put on hold especially when you're putting them on hold to address someone else's problem. Unfortunately, there are circumstances when this is unavoidable.

If you have to ask a customer to hold, ask them first. In some circumstances, they might not have the time to wait and would prefer to call back later. Instead say, "May I place you on a brief hold while I do XYZ?"

If the hold is taking longer than anticipated, hop back on to let them know you appreciate their patience. Explain the situation and reset their expectations.

8. I Don't Have Any Record Of Your Purchase/Account

Want to send a customer over the edge? Say this. There's nothing more frustrating than reaching out for help only to be met with disorganization on the other end.

If you find yourself leaning on this phrase a lot, your company will likely benefit from investing in some customer service or customer success software. Software like this has the ability to increase transparency and collaboration across departments, so you're never left at a loss when you realize the notes from the customer's last call are hiding in your colleague's inbox.

9. That's not something I can do

Even if a customer's request exceeds your pay grade or permissions, it's still your responsibility to direct them towards a solution.

And don't forget to think back to #3 on this one: In most cases, this phrase can be prevented by surfacing the negative impact that these type of role restrictions cause with your senior management. Perhaps there's room to create more flexible permissions to avoid having to climb the ladder every time you need to perform a certain task for a customer.

Remember: We're All Human

Being in a customer-facing role can be tasking especially when you're not equipped with the proper tools and permissions to help a customer quickly get to a solution. Luckily, you're in control of how you choose to respond.

This isn't to say that you should constantly feel like you're walking on eggshells, but you should be conscious and strategic with how you handle customer communications. Put yourself in the shoes of the person on the other end of the line, and show some empathy, it'll go a long way.

5

IMPORTANCE OF EMPOWERING YOUR CUSTOMER CONTACT STAFF

Successful organisations recognise that in order to provide great customer service, they need to give the same level of attention and focus to their employees, as they do to their customers.

Behaviour breeds behaviour. So to increase the probability of achieving customer satisfaction, you need employees who value and are highly skilled in customer service.

Research shows that employees in sales and customer service roles who are emotionally intelligent are better equipped to provide high levels of customer service. However, providing your employees with the right support and environment will help you achieve a successful business. Here are some tips:

TREAT STAFF AS YOU TREAT YOUR CUSTOMERS

Be transparent in all your communications, keeping them fully informed of changes, respecting their views and opinions and placing a high value on the work of customer service staff. This could also involve letting your staff sample your service and products, in recognition of their hard work and commitment.

PAY ATTENTION TO THOSE WHO DON'T SERVE CUSTOMERS DIRECTLY

Chances are, if they're not serving a customer, they're serving someone who is, and these people are their 'internal' customers.

Are they focused on the needs of the external customer and supporting those that directly interact with them? Or are they giving priority and assigning more value to internal processes and tasks?

Build a team culture where everyone recognises their role in providing great customer service.

Every team member is a link in the service chain, meaning that it only takes one team member to break or spoil the customer experience.

LOOK FOR AND RECOGNISE OUTSTANDING CUSTOMER SERVICE

A genuine 'thank you' or 'well done' goes a long way in recognising an employee's valuable contribution to great customer service.

A simple gift that the employee will value and can be given to the employee within 48 hours of demonstrating the outstanding service works best. For example, a gift voucher, or a bunch of flowers, that the line manager can give out to say 'thank you'.

Consider using an award scheme where individuals, colleagues and customers can nominate those who demonstrate exceptional levels of customer service. Make the nomination process easy, fast, accessible and appropriate to the way your employees and customers communicate with you e.g. notice board, daily briefings, web site, intranet, voice-mail and email.

RECRUIT AND MEASURE PERFORMANCE AROUND CUSTOMER-ORIENTATED BEHAVIOURS

Do this from the initial recruitment stage, through to the annual performance appraisal. Are you measuring the right customer orientated behaviours and attitudes that achieve high levels of customer service within your selection process?

SET MEASURABLE OBJECTIVES AROUND CREATING/MAINTAINING EXCEPTIONAL CUSTOMER SERVICE

Quality assessment is also a good technique, scoring the customer service rep based on their conversation with the customer. Remember to cascade them across the organisation, so that everyone can see how they are all contributing to your business strategy and goals, including where they could support each other.

REVIEW INDIVIDUAL PERFORMANCE REGULARLY

Undertake performance reviews, not just during the annual appraisal. Give feedback about what's going well, as well as providing coaching for areas needing development.

CHECK THE DIVERSITY OF YOUR EMPLOYEES TO SEE IF THEY REFLECT YOUR CUSTOMER BASE

Your employees are likely to 'connect' and 'engage' more readily with your customers if they fully appreciate their background, values and culture. Where this is not practical, provide them with some diversity awareness training to really help them appreciate your customers needs.

HOLD DAILY OR WEEKLY BRIEFING SESSIONS

This allows employees communicating with customers to ensure they remain up to date with the business products and services. A standing 10 to 15 minute briefing will be good, enabling you to review any service issues from the day or week before.

HAVE REGULAR CUSTOMER SERVICE SESSIONS WITH STAFF

They'll have lots of ideas on how things could be improved. Encourage them to think of what can be done to provide the 'wow factor'. Use the creativity of the group to brainstorm and think outside the box for less obvious suggestions. Recognise and reward the best ideas.

COACH TEAM MEMBERS

This will help to bring the highest level of performance and commitment to those looking after the customers.

UCHE AKEEB

CONCLUSION

Customer service goes a long way these days, and sets you apart from your competitors in a price-dominated marketplace. Exceptional and consistent customer service is what makes one operation more successful than the other. The funny thing about this is that good customer service costs an operation next to nothing and brings more value and continued business relationships to the table.

Our customers today want to know that they are dealing with the best: a company that goes that extra mile to make sure their needs are not only met but exceeded, and that issues are anticipated before they become issues. Yes, a clean product delivered at a competitive price day in and day out does mean something, but the simple things like saying "Thank you" for the business, straightening up the shelves, or proactively following up goes a long way toward customer retention.

Today, we are seeing that, more often than not, exceptional customer service makes the infrequent issues not as painful as they once were. Our customers expect and deserve the best, and consistent excellent customer service helps to generate not only customer retention and renewals, but also referrals.

It is good to note that: Feedback and reviews are also vital for the company because they provide valuable information and allow companies to determine what works for their consumers and what does not. It is good to Learn from your customers' feedback and improve your customer service.

More and more managers are playing an active role in making sure their staff expresses and practices good customer-service actions on a daily basis.

By training staff on the importance of going that extra mile and leading by example, many operations are able to increase sales based upon word of mouth rather than an expansion of the sales team. Remember, it costs almost nothing and pays well.

REFERENCES

Zemke, R. & Woods, J. A. (1999). Best Practices in Customer Service

Barlow, J. & Paul S. (2006). Branded Customer Service: The New Competitive Edge

Gillen, T. (1990). 20 Training Workshops for Customer Service, Vol. 1

Cook, S. (2008). Customer Care Excellence: How to create an effective customer focus, 5th edition.

Goodman, J. A (2009). Strategic Customer Service

THE IMPACT OF EXCELLENT CUSTOMER SERVICE ON BUSINESS GROWTH

www.ingramcontent.com/pod-product-compliance
Lightning Source LLC
Chambersburg PA
CBHW020456220526
45464CB00002B/1006